HOW TO WRITE CASH GENERATING GRANT PROPOSALS

by

Lawrence V. Stefanile

How to Write Cash Generating Grant Proposals

HOW TO WRITE CASH GENERATING GRANT PROPOSALS

ISBN – 13:978-1519537850
ISBN - 1519537859

How to Write Cash Generating Grant Proposals
Copyright 2015 by Lawrence V. Stefanile
No portion of this manual, either written or e-book may be used or reproduced in any manner whatsoever without written permission except in the case of brief quotations embodied in critical articles or reviews

First Edition
December 2015

How to Write Cash Generating Grant Proposals

CONTENTS

∎

Introduction	1
Key Terms	2
Preface	3
Step One: The Prospective Grantor	4 - 5
Step Two: Applying for a Grant	6
Step Three: Contacting the Grantor	7
Step Four: Reviewing the Application Manual	8
Step Five: Preparing the Letter of Intent	9
Step Six: Collecting Relevant Information	10 - 11
Step Seven: Drafting the Grant Proposal	12 - 13
Step Eight: Project Justification	14
Step Nine: Project Description	15
Step Ten: Project Budget	16
Step Eleven: Reviewing the Application	17 - 18
Step Twelve: Drafting the Cover Letter	19 - 20
Appendix A – Sample Letter of Intent	21
Appendix B – Sample Project Justification	22 - 23
Appendix C – Sample Project Description	24
Appendix D – Sample Project Budget	25
Appendix E – Sample Cover Letter	26
Congratulations	27
Grant Administration Guide Coming Soon	28

How to Write Cash Generating Grant Proposals

INTRODUCTION

■

With shrinking dollars available for philanthropic purposes and contracting government funding programs too many worthwhile grant proposals gather dust that could have been funded had they demonstrated a built-in competitive edge.

Following successful careers in higher education and health care fundraising over three decades ago, I founded and manage a consulting firm dedicated to generating funding for clients in the municipal and non-profit sectors of our economy. In those years, I have researched, developed and submitted grant applications to federal and state agencies and corporate foundations that have produced multiple millions of dollars for a vast array of projects, including civic center, hospital building and barrier free construction, energy conservation, recreational site development, sensitive lands acquisitions, roads and infrastructure development, to name a few.

There is no mystery to the preparation of successful grant proposals. In order to achieve a competitive edge, it takes diligence, organization and writing your proposals in concise descriptive prose consistent with the requirements and award criteria of potential grantors.

Throughout this text, I have highlighted in bold lettering, key terms to provide the reader an ease of review.

How to Write Cash Generating Grant Proposals

KEY TERMS

■

Request for Proposal (RFP)
Grantor
Grant Developer
Municipal Manager
Project Officer
Letter of Intent
Application Manual
Application Checklist
Quality Control Assessment
Grant Program Rules and Procedures
Grant Proposal Selection Criteria
Municipal Engineer
Municipal Planner
Master Plan
City Council
Finance Manager
Tax Assessor
Legal Counsel
Project Justification
Project Features
Project Benefits
Project Description
Project Budget
Cover Letter
Award Letter

How to Write Cash Generating Grant Proposals

PREFACE

■

This guide focuses on municipalities seeking funding to bring worthwhile projects into reality. The example presented herein is a grant application developed by a newly hired **Municipal Grant Developer** and submitted by her municipality to rehabilitate its declining baseball field, thereby expanding active recreational opportunities.

The application is invited by a state agency as a **Request for Proposal (RFP),** which simply means the granting authority has requested applications for review on a competitive basis for a limited amount of available funds pursuant to a specific goal. Although a capital construction example, the principles employed are transferrable to other types of special purpose grant applications.

Following is a step-by-step process I have used throughout the years in developing a myriad of successful grant proposals that resulted in funding thousands of much needed municipal and non-profit projects that without the external financing of government agencies and philanthropic foundations would not have seen the light of day.

Let's get started.

STEP ONE

The Prospective Grantor
(*Hereafter referred to as Grantor*)

■

The **Grantor** can make your project happen. It might be a government (federal, state or county) agency, legislatively empowered, or a corporate or individually funded foundation with specific philanthropic purposes. When I started my career as a college development officer (in the days before the Internet), I made frequent calls to federal, state and county agencies and traveled to the Foundation Library in New York City to research and develop lists of potential grantors that might benefit my employer. The process is more efficient today, thanks to the Internet. The information I culled manually then can now be obtained electronically and in the comfort of your office.

This guide is the first in a series; soon the following guides will be available:

- Administering Grant Awards
- Researching Prospective Grantors
- Establishing and Managing Grantor Networks

While this guide focuses on a step-by-step approach to preparing cash generating grant proposals, following are some tips to help you to identify grantors whose missions, philosophies and goals are consistent with your projects.

How to Write Cash Generating Grant Proposals

- Google: Foundation Grant Opportunities

- Google: Grant Opportunities for your state, e.g. Grant Opportunities – California

- Google: The Catalog of Federal Domestic Assistance Programs

- Contact the Governor's Office of your respective state (whose phone numbers are readily available on the Internet) and request information on available state grants

STEP TWO

Applying for a Grant

■

Congratulations, Mary Lime. You have been appointed **Municipal Grant Developer** for Any Town, a mid-size municipality in Any State. After accepting kudos and the sense of euphoria you feel at winning the appointment, Margaret Brown, **Municipal Manager** informs you of your first project, the rehabilitation of a baseball field with an estimated price tag of $100,000. She provides an overview of the project and hands you the phone number of the potential grantor, a state agency that makes grants on a competitive basis whose purpose it is to expand and increase active recreational opportunities to the public, such as the baseball field rehabilitation project under consideration by the town council. She explains that the rehabilitation of the baseball field is high priority within the local government and community. She informs you that a grant that is half of the estimated cost is needed for the project to move forward. The mini-panic you experience is transient and your first order of business is to contact the prospective grantor's project officer and get the project underway.

STEP THREE

Contacting the Grantor

■

You settle into your new office, review the features of the project provided by Margaret Brown for which you will seek funding. Now, you are set to go. You take a deep breath; pick up the phone and dial the grantor's **Project Officer** at the phone number provided you by the **Municipal Manager**. He answers his phone on the second ring identifying himself as John Green. You identify yourself, and referring to your notes you describe your project and the purpose of your call. He is cordial, informative and generous with his time. You feel at ease. Based on the information you supply, and that you represent an incorporated municipality John Green determines your project meets the **Grantor's** eligibility requirements to apply for a grant. He informs you that a **Letter of Intent** to apply for funds from the **Municipal Manager** is required to trigger the application process. He takes your email address and promises to send to you an **Application Manual** that contains forms, instructions and an **Application Checklist**. You hang up the phone and breathe a sigh of relief. You did well, you made your first contact and the grant application process is launched. You turn on your computer and open your email. As promised, the **Application Manual** from the **Project Officer** is there in bold letters awaiting your attention. By email, you acknowledge its receipt to the project officer, with whom you will stay in touch to resolve questions and seek clarifications throughout the application process. You print the manual. You are now ready to move to the next step.

STEP FOUR

Reviewing the Application Manual

■

The **Application Manual** is your roadmap to the preparation of cash generating grant proposals. It consists of **Program Rules and Procedures**, a series of application forms and importantly, the **Grant Proposal Selection Criteria** *(hereafter referred to as **Selection Criteria**)*, which you will use as a filter when preparing the description of your project. A green marker in hand, you delve into the manual highlighting those relevant statements that apply to the development of your application for funding, such as the source of grant funds, eligible and ineligible items for funding, and the applicant requirement to commit half of the project cost available in capital funds to match the grant amount of a successful application. You underscore the submission deadline and that a completed application can be submitted electronically or by regular mail. You record in your file, the respective email and regular mail addresses.

▶ Examine the **Grant Program Rules and Procedures** diligently, with emphasis on eligible and ineligible funding items, if only for a single practical reason. The last thing any **Grant Developer** wants to experience is submitting an application requesting funding for ineligible budget line items, which would result in the application's disapproval and rejection by the grantor.

STEP FIVE

Preparing the Letter of Intent

■

Following the instructions contained in the **Application Manual** and your discussion with the **Project Officer**, you draft a **Letter of Intent** to apply for project funding for the municipality's baseball field rehabilitation for the **Municipal Manager's** signature.

In the Letter of Intent you have drafted -

- **The Municipal Manager**

    ✓ Verifies your contact with the **Project Officer** who has invited the submission of the municipality's **Letter of Intent** to apply for funds dedicated to the rehabilitation of its baseball field.

    ✓ Approves and signs your draft and returns it to you for mailing.

- You email or send the **Letter of Intent** by regular mail to the grantor's **Project Officer** with a copy to the **Municipal Manager.**

Refer to Appendix A

Sample Letter of Intent

STEP SIX

Collecting Relevant Information

■

It is now time to identify within the municipal government information sources and collect from each the data and information needed to develop your cash generating grant proposal. Since this example is a capital project involving the rehabilitation of a municipally owned facility you interview the following colleagues who will provide you the information required to develop your persuasive grant proposal:

- **Municipal Engineer** who pursuant to your interview questions, as follow: describes the field's conceptual plan, its dimensions and existing conditions, the field's surface defects, environmental factors and the engineer's construction plan to rehabilitate the field by eliminating its deficits and the associated estimated line item budget.

- **Municipal Planner** verifies that the project is consistent with the municipality's **Master Plan** and indicates the relevant sections of the plan.

- **Finance Manager** affirms that half of the engineer's projected total cost is available in a capital account for the project.

- **Tax Assessor** who provides you a tax map showing the field's location.

How to Write Cash Generating Grant Proposals

- **Legal Counsel** who prepares an endorsing resolution from the template provided in the **Application Manual** for introduction and passage at a public hearing of the town council fulfilling the grantor's requirement.

STEP SEVEN

Drafting the Grant Proposal

Grant proposals are sales pitches. A persuasive grant proposal should be structured in such a way that grantors are influenced to invest in your project by underwriting a portion of its associated costs. In organizing your grant proposal it is important that you recognize the difference between features and benefits and how their synergistic application will increase the odds of achieving your desired result.

▶ **Features** describe elements of your project. In our example, a feature of the project might be: upon project completion the grass outfield will be a beautiful emerald green color. By itself, feature selling is generally ineffective, because it doesn't address the underlying problem or problems that need to be resolved consistent with the grantor's selection criteria.

▶ **Benefits** describe project features, but with an added significant dimension, the benefit is tied to the feature demonstrating an improvement in the current situation. In our example your proposal might say: the resurfaced outfield complemented by a beautiful emerald green grass field will contribute to fewer player injuries thereby achieving conformance with the grantor's selection criteria.

How to Write Cash Generating Grant Proposals

You are now equipped with comprehensive detailed information needed to begin the development of your grant application. You thoroughly review the grantor's **Selection Criteria**. You photocopy the application form contained in the **Application Manual** and insert in designated spaces the requested information and begin developing your preliminary draft, including names, addresses, telephone number and email address of the town, **Municipal Manager** and **Grant Developer**, location of the baseball field according to the tax map, the project budget showing the amount of the grant requested and the municipality's match from its capital budget and an abstract of the project.

STEP EIGHT

Project Justification

■

Why should a grantor underwrite 50% of your project cost with taxpayer funds? Good question. You must provide in your proposal a persuasive justification for the grantor's financial participation in your project. Your initial impulse is to declare that the town possesses only half of the estimated cost and without external funding the project cannot become reality. As true as this statement is, by itself, it is not persuasive enough for the grantor to open its cash register and dedicate funds to your project. The municipality's financial condition is a single element in the process. Your justification must go beyond financial need. This is where your analysis of the **Municipal Engineer's** description of the elements of the project comes into play.

You evaluate the notes you took during your meeting with the **Municipal Engineer**. The intrinsic need and purpose for the rehabilitation of the baseball field consistent with the **Selection Criteria** now comes into sharp focus. You see the **Grantor** is interested in investing in a project that will expand and increase active recreation pursuits and improve the quality of play, safety and environmental conditions in order to achieve that goal.

Your next step is on the horizon. You are excited to move in its direction realizing when project features are wed to benefits a winning formula has been achieved.

Refer to Appendix B
Sample Project Justification

STEP NINE

Project Description

■

The **Application Manual** asks that you provide a detailed description of the actual improvements for which your application seeks funding. It requires specific explications of the exact work that will take place in the baseball field, each element building to a comprehensive picture of the completed project. Here you refer to the notes you took during your meeting with the **Municipal Engineer.**

▶ It is important to link each element of work in your project description to the **Municipal Engineer's** line item budget. In so doing, you create a clear picture of the comprehensive rehabilitation of the baseball field and the funding that will make it a reality consistent with the grantor's mission and goals.

Refer to Appendix C
Sample Project Description

STEP TEN

Project Budget

■

The **Project Budget** describes the allocation of costs on a line item basis. You review the several items making up the baseball field rehabilitation, and key each to its respective budget line item to assure that statements in your project description are linked to estimated costs. For example, your project narrative describes the installation of a safety net that will afford protection from foul balls to spectators; the project budget lists a line item of $15,000. You have accomplished that which the grantor looks for in its evaluation, i.e. the linkage of construction elements to budgetary costs representing an as-built rehabilitated baseball field.

▶ It is important that all elements of project construction outlined in your **Project Description** link to their associated costs.

Refer to Appendix D
Sample Project Budget

STEP ELEVEN

Reviewing Your Application

■

Congratulations!

You have completed a preliminary draft of the municipality's application, with all of the required attachments cited in the **Application Manual**, including tax map, photographs of the baseball field, engineer's sketch and budget of the rehabilitated field, and the Council's resolution requesting a grant of $50,000 for the field's rehabilitation. You did one other thing, while not required was a perceptive marketing move on your part. With the authorization of the **Municipal Manager**, you described the project to the public in an issue of the municipal newsletter concluding with a request for letters supporting the project. Several letters enthusiastically supporting the project were received. You attached them to your application, which demonstrated community involvement and strengthened the application's appeal to the **Grantor**. Before presenting it for certifying signatures by the **Municipal Manager** and filing it with the **Grantor**, you perform a **Quality Control Assessment** (that's a fancy way of saying you double-check your work to assure its completion and accuracy).

Here's what you do.

- Assure the application's completeness by using the **Application Checklist** as your guide. Upon review, you find all items of information requested in the checklist have been noted. Your application is 100% complete.

- Re-visit the **Selection Criteria**, which guided you throughout the application development process. Upon review, you are confident that your project's content is consistent with the **Selection Criteria** and should rank high enough to be competitive for the grant sought.

STEP TWELVE

Drafting the Cover Letter and Submitting the Application

■

The **Cover Letter** (sometimes known as a transmittal letter) that is directed to the **Grantor's Project Officer** captures all items contained in your application. You compose it for the **Municipal Manager's** signature with copies to all of your colleagues that contributed to the development of your application and the elected governing body

- Prior to composing the cover letter, jot down, in sequential order all items comprising your application.

- With the above information at hand, you are ready to begin drafting the cover letter.

- Open your word processor and begin typing.

- Using either a block or indent format, type in the date, and then the name and address of the **Grantor's Project Officer.**

- Following those style requirements, in sequence type in those items comprising your application.

- Conclude the letter with a space for the **Municipal Manager's** signature.

How to Write Cash Generating Grant Proposals

- Show the names of those to receive copies of the cover letter following the **Municipal Manager's** signature.

- The **Cover Letter** provides you with another opportunity (we'll call it a triple-check) to perform another quality control assessment.

- Send to the **Grantor** (electronically or by regular mail) the completed application with attachments transmitted by the **Municipal Manager's** cover letter and obtain an acknowledgement of its receipt.

- Congratulations! You have completed and submitted a persuasive application to obtain $50,000 dedicated to a high priority municipal project.

Refer to Appendix E

Sample Cover Letter

APPENDIX A

Sample Letter of Intent to Apply for Funding

■

November 1, 2015

John Green, Project Officer
Recreation and Conservation Department
Any State
State Plaza
Any Capitol, Any State, Zip Code

Dear Mr. Green:

This letter is follow-up to your recent telephone discussion with Mary Lime, Any Town's Grant Developer concerning our interest in submitting a grant proposal for the rehabilitation of our baseball field. Ms. Lime has informed me that based on your discussion our project is eligible for consideration. Please accept this correspondence as our Letter of Intent to apply for funds for our baseball field rehabilitation project.

Thank you for your consideration.

Sincerely yours,

Margaret Brown, Municipal Manager

cc: Municipal Council
       Mary Lime, Grant Developer

APPENDIX B
Sample Project Justification

∎

The Baseball Field Rehabilitation Project is a high priority within Any Town garnering substantial community support. It addresses the need to eliminate unsafe conditions on the playing field resulting from soil erosion and topographical unevenness caused by a dangerous decline where the infield and outfield meet. This condition has resulted in player falls and ankle injuries, and has compromised safety and the quality of play. Today, television and newspapers report on an almost regular basis spectators dodging and being hit by foul balls and splintered bats. This project deals with that issue by installing a safety net that will significantly reduce the number of foul balls reaching spectators thereby averting injuries. Old and worn infield equipment on the diamond will be replaced to enhance the quality of play and reduce shoe jamming when players run from base to base. Equally spaced ten-foot high shade trees along the outfield's chain link fence will achieve an aesthetic buffer against the view of a busy traffic corridor. Upon completion of surface re-grading and topsoiling the outfield will be replanted with a hearty natural grass seed and the diamond with an infield clay mix, both with extended lives. Due to the existing condition of the field the town has been unable to host regional tournaments and off-season recreational activities on the field. Funding our project is consistent with the department's selection criteria to provide a safe playing area and encourage expanded facility use while attracting greater passive participation in the sport.

Analysis:

The **Project Justification** identifies conditions that will be resolved, i.e. the **Benefits** of the project that are consistent with the **Grantor's Selection Criteria**, including:

a. Improving safety during play
b. Enhancing spectator safety
c. Increasing utilization of the facility
d. Linking each element of construction to project description and budget line items
e. Demonstrating consistency with grantor goals and objectives

APPENDIX C
Sample Project Description

■

Following is a detailed description of proposed improvements to Any Town's Baseball Improvement Project for which grant funding shall be dedicated. Grading improvements to the infield and sections of the outfield shall be implemented to resolve unevenness at the juncture of the infield and outfield. Clay and grass within the areas of grading will be restored with products having extended lives. A safety netting system will be installed behind home plate and along the third baseline to limit the number of foul balls being hit into the spectator stands. The infield rehabilitation includes replacement of worn bases. Equally spaced ten-foot high shade trees will be planted along the periphery of the outfield fence to create an aesthetic environmental addition to the playing field buffering the highway traffic in the view of center field. This project will have a minimum service life of ten years and is consistent with all applicable barrier-free regulations.

Analysis

 a. Describes each element of construction
 b. Specifies improvements each element of construction will produce
 c. Identifies extended life of the project upon completion
 d. Introduced an environmental buffer
 e. Links each element of construction to the project justification and budget

APPENDIX D

Sample Project Budget

■

Item #	Description	Total Amount
1	Soil Erosion Control Measures	$ 4,000.00
2	Site Clearance	16,000.00
3	Infield Clay Mix	23,000.00
4	Safety Netting System 30' High	28,000.00
5	Top Soil, 4" Thick	6,000.00
6	Grass Sodding	12,000.00
7	Baseball Bases	4,000.00
8	Shade Trees/Planting 10' Tall	7,000.00
	Total	$ 100,000.00

Note:

Engineering design and inspection services for this project are provided by Any Town's in-house engineering department personnel, which costs are borne by the municipality.

APPENDIX E
Sample Cover Letter

November 15, 2015

John Green, Project Officer
Recreation and Conservation Department
Any State - State Plaza
Any Capitol, Any State, Zip Code

Dear Mr. Green:

Enclosed is one (1) complete certified application for Any Town's baseball field rehabilitation project, including the following attachments.

1. Municipal Program Park Improvement Application
2. Tax Map and Aerial Location of Project
3. Existing Field Dimensions
4. Color Site Photographs
5. Certified Municipal Resolution
6. Project Budget
7. Municipal Planner's letter attesting to consistency of project with Village Master Plan
8. Projected Project Construction Schedule

Please contact the undersigned person should there be any questions.

Sincerely,

Margaret Brown, Municipal Manager

cc: Municipal Council Municipal Planner
Mary Lime, Grant Developer Finance Manager
Municipal Engineer Municipal Attorney

CONGRATULATIONS

Your intercom buzzes.

Margaret Brown, **Municipal Manager** is calling to inform and congratulate you that an **Award Letter** has been received from the Governor's Office informing the Municipal Council that a grant of $50,000 to defray half of the construction cost of the Municipal Baseball Field Rehabilitation Project has been awarded. You are elated, as you should be. Ms. Brown says she will send a copy of the award letter with the **Grant Administration Manual** to you and requests you begin its review and report to her on the procedures to be followed to assure compliance with grantor regulations and collect the grant funds.

How to Write Cash Generating Grant Proposals

GRANT ADMINISTRATION GUIDE COMING SOON

Will Show How to:

- Establish contact with grantor administrators
- Prepare for pre-construction conferences
- Coordinate project construction activities
- Prepare post-construction certification form
- Prepare project grant reimbursement request form

www.ingramcontent.com/pod-product-compliance
Lightning Source LLC
Chambersburg PA
CBHW020715180526
45163CB00008B/3104